MY WORLD OF SCIENCE

# Water

### Revised and Updated

Angela Royston

**www.heinemann.co.uk/library**
Visit our website to find out more information about Heinemann Library books.

To order:
☎ Phone 44 (0) 1865 888066
▤ Send a fax to 44 (0) 1865 314091
▯ Visit the Heinemann Bookshop at www.heinemann.co.uk/library to browse our catalogue and order online.

First published in Great Britain by Heinemann Library, Halley Court, Jordan Hill, Oxford OX2 8EJ, part of Pearson Education. Heinemann is a registered trademark of Pearson Education Ltd.

Editorial: Diyan Leake
Design: Joanna Hinton-Malivoire
Picture research: Melissa Allison and Mica Brancic
Production: Alison Parsons

Originated by Chroma Graphics (Overseas) Pte Ltd
Printed and bound in China by South China Printing Co. Ltd

ISBN 978 0 431 13760 5 (hardback)
12 11 10 09 08
10 9 8 7 6 5 4 3 2 1

ISBN 978 0 431 13784 1 (paperback)
12 11 10 09 08
10 9 8 7 6 5 4 3 2 1

**British Library Cataloguing in Publication Data**
Royston, Angela
Water. – New ed. – (My world of science)
 1. Water – Juvenile literature
 I. Title
 553.7

**Acknowledgements**
The publishers would like to thank the following for permission to reproduce photographs: © Alamy p. **21** (Barry Lewis); © Corbis pp. **5, 6, 7, 8, 11** (First Light), **14, 15, 17, 24, 27**; © Eye Ubiquitous p. **18**; © Getty Images/Stone pp. **20, 28**; © Robert Harding p. **29**; © Still Pictures p. **25** (Toby Adamson); © Trevor Clifford pp. **4, 9, 10, 12, 13, 16, 19, 22, 23, 26**.

Cover photograph reproduced with permission of © Getty Images (Photonic/VEER Brian Fraunfelter).

The publishers would like to thank Jon Bliss for his assistance in the preparation of this book.

Every effort has been made to contact copyright holders of any material reproduced in this book. Any omissions will be rectified in subsequent printings if notice is given to the publishers.

# Contents

Any words appearing in the text in bold, **like this**, are explained in the glossary.

# What is water?

Water is usually a liquid. A liquid does not have a shape of its own. It takes the shape of its **container**. Which of these containers holds the least water? (Answer on page 31.)

Sometimes you can see water, steam, and ice all in the same place.

Water is a clear, runny liquid. But water can also be a solid piece of ice and steam in the air. Ice is very cold, and steam is very hot.

# Where water comes from

When it rains, water **flows** off the land into streams and rivers. Streams and rivers flow across the land into the sea.

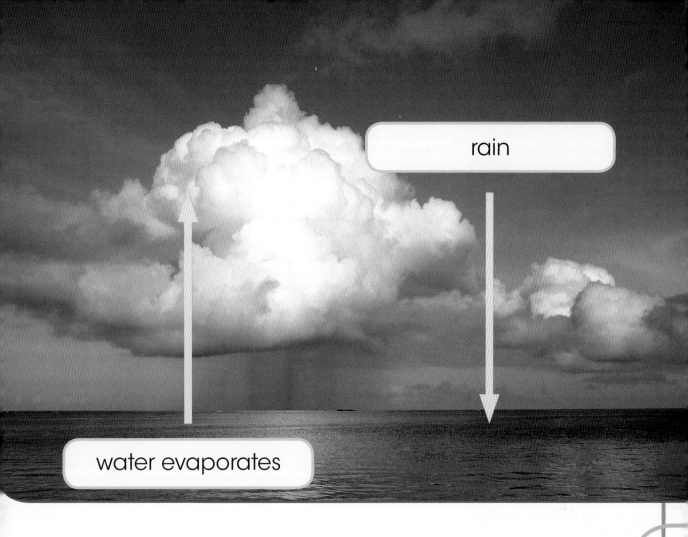

rain

water evaporates

Some of the water in the sea and in rivers **evaporates**. This means it changes into gas called water vapour. This gas floats into the air and forms new rain clouds.

# Water for life

People, plants, and animals all need
water to stay alive. Some farmers spray
their plants with water to make them
grow better.

The juice in oranges is mainly water.

All food has water in it. Fruit and vegetables have lots of water in them. Squeeze an orange to see how much juice you can get.

# Using water

We use water at home for washing clothes, dishes, ourselves, and other things. Soap makes things easier to wash.

hosepipe

Firefighters use water to put out fires. They pump the water on to the flames through long hosepipes.

# Flowing water

Water always tries to **flow** downhill. The **steeper** the slope, the faster water flows. What will happen if this girl tips the bottle more? (Answer on page 31.)

Water cannot flow uphill on its own. When you drink through a straw, you have to suck the water up into your mouth.

# Ice and water

When water becomes very cold, it changes into ice. Ice is a solid and so it keeps its shape.

This statue has been cut from a huge block of ice.

**Thermometers** measure **temperature** in degrees. Water always freezes at 0 degrees **Celsius**, and ice melts when the temperature is more than 0 degrees.

# Heating water

When water is heated, it slowly turns into gas. Water is at its **boiling point** when it reaches 100 degrees **Celsius**. Be careful – boiling water **scalds**.

Bubbles of gas form in the water. The bubbles rise to the top of the water and burst. The gas drifts up into the air.

# Steam

You cannot see the gas in the air, but you can see steam. Steam is made when water gas turns back into tiny water **droplets**.

Mist often forms on mirrors and windows.

Water droplets form at other times too. If you breathe on to a mirror, it will become misty. The mist is made of tiny water droplets.

# Drying

Wet hair can be dried with a hairdrier. The water in your hair slowly changes into gas. The gas drifts into the air and your hair dries.

As puddles dry, they get smaller. Try measuring a puddle after the rain on a warm day. Measure it again every 20 minutes. See how small it gets.

# Floating and sinking

Some things are very light. They float
when you put them into water. You can
test different things to see which ones
will float.

The heavy things will sink to the bottom of the bowl. Which of these things were too heavy to float? (Answer on page 31.)

# Light for its size

Something floats if it is light for its size. This ship is big and heavy and yet it floats. That is because the weight of the ship is spread out over the water.

These heavy logs are floating on the
river. Wood floats because there is lots of
air trapped inside it.

# Water pushes back

When you put something into water, it pushes some of the water away. The water then pushes back! This balloon is difficult to push under the water.

When you lie on water, the water pushes up and makes you float. This is just like when the water pushes back against a balloon.

Spreading yourself out helps you float.

# Moving through water

When you swim, you pull the water backwards and the water pushes you forwards. The force of your stroke pushes you forwards.

Boats also move forwards by pulling
the water backwards. These people pull
the paddles back to push the canoes
forwards. Moving through water is fun!

# Glossary

**boiling point** the temperature at which a liquid begins to boil

**Celsius** scale for measuring temperature

**container** something that you can put things in – for example, a box or jar

**droplet** very small drop

**evaporate** when liquid water changes into gas

**flow** move smoothly

**scald** burn with very hot water or steam

**steep** rises or falls sharply

**temperature** how hot or cold something is

**thermometer** tool for measuring temperature

# Answers

**Page 4 –** The tallest, thin glass holds the least water.

**Page 12 –** The water will flow faster if the girl tips the bottle more.

**Page 23 –** The shell, keys, and buttons were too heavy to float.

# More books to read

*A Drop in the Ocean: The Story of Water,* Jacqui Bailey (A&C Black, 2004)

*The Drop Goes Plop: A First Look at the Water Cycle,* Sam Godwin (Picture Window Books, 2004)

*Using Materials: How We Use Water,* Chris Oxlade (Raintree, 2005)

# Index